recycling & reusing

Glass

Ruth Thomson

Photography by Neil Thomson

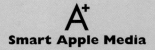

Smart Apple Media

First published in 2006 by Franklin Watts
338 Euston Road, London NW1 3BH

Franklin Watts Australia, Hachette Children's Books
Level 17/207 Kent Street, Sydney NSW 2000

Series editor: Rachel Cooke, Series designer: Holly Mann, Art Director: Rachel Hamdi,
Consultants: Jo Hollins, Education Officer at Rockware Glass and Ben Stone,
Recycling Officer at British Glass

Additional Photographs
Madeleine Boulesteix: 19 (top); Dichrolicious (Richard and Diana Sewell): 18 (bottom); Green Bottle
Unit: 27; Rockware Glass: 8 (center), 22- 23; Recycle now: front and back endpapers, 12 (top), 20
(bottom left), 21 (left)

Published in the United States by Smart Apple Media
2140 Howard Drive West, North Mankato, Minnesota 56003

Library of Congress Cataloging-in-Publication Data

Thomson, Ruth, 1949-
Glass / by Ruth Thomson.
p. cm. – (Recycling and reusing)
Includes index.
ISBN-13: 978-1-58340-942-8
1. Glass waste—Recycling—Juvenile literature. 2. Glass—Juvenile literature.
I. Title.

TP859.7.T56 2006
666'.14—dc22   2006000022

9 8 7 6 5 4 3 2 1

Contents

What is glass like?

It is easy to see why glass is such a useful **material**.
Almost everywhere you look—at home, at school, or
in the street—you can spot things made of glass.

Glass is see-through.
It lets in light but keeps out
wind and rain.

Glass does not become soggy
or leak when it gets wet.
That's why glass bottles are useful for
storing **liquids** such as juice and oil.

A lens is made of curved glass. It is thicker in the middle than around the edges. This bends light to make things look bigger than they really are.

Glass is hard and smooth. It is easy to clean, so it is safe and **hygienic** for drinks and food.

IT'S A FACT

A mirror is made of a smooth glass sheet with a thin layer of shiny silver on the back. Light hitting a mirror bounces back to show your reflection.

Glass does not mix with or change anything it touches. Food in sealed glass jars stays fresh for a long time.

Oops!

Glass cracks or shatters if it is hit or dropped. **Be careful!** Broken glass has very sharp edges.

Making new glass

Glass is produced in a **factory**. It is not a **natural material**.

The raw ingredients

Glass is made mostly of pure sand called silica. This is mixed with limestone and soda ash and heated in a **furnace** to 2,900 °F (1,600 °C).

silica sand

soda ash (a chemical)

limestone (crushed, chalky rock)

The inside of a furnace

amber cullet

green cullet

clear cullet

Soda ash lowers the melting **temperature** of the sand. Limestone makes the glass stronger. Some **cullet** (crushed, recycled glass) is also added. This is of the same type and color as the finished glass. It helps the mixture **melt** more quickly.

8

Poured, pressed, and pulled

Molten glass is hot, soft, and flexible. It can be poured, blown, pressed, pulled, or put in a **mold** to make almost any shape.

handblown jug

molded jar

IT'S A FACT

Scientists call glass a "super cooled liquid," because it acts like a liquid. Although glass feels completely solid at room temperature, it becomes runny when it is heated. Light passes through glass, just as it does through a clear liquid.

Once glass has been shaped, it is left to cool. As it cools, glass becomes hard and strong and stays in its particular shape.

LOOK AND SEE

How many different glass jars can you find? The shapes help products to stand out from one another.

Returning glass bottles

Most empty glass jars and bottles are thrown away. However, getting rid of glass is a problem.

Burn, bury, or break down?

Glass cannot be burned. If it is buried at a **landfill site**, it takes up a lot of space. Glass does not **rot**, so it also spoils the **environment**. Since it is easy to wash glass and use it again and again, it is a real waste to throw it away.

Back to sender

Some companies sell soft drinks to shops, cafés, and bars in returnable glass bottles.

They collect the empty bottles and return them to a bottling plant to be washed, **sterilized**, refilled, labeled, capped, and sold again.

Why reuse glass?

Reusing glass bottles uses less **energy** than melting old bottles to make new ones or making new bottles from scratch.

A fair exchange

In some places, you cannot buy a new bottled drink unless you bring back an empty bottle in exchange.

In other places—for example, in this Egyptian shop—you pay an extra amount for the bottle.

This is called a deposit. When you return the empty bottle, you get the deposit back.

Reusing glass

We should save glass jars and bottles whenever we can.

Use it again

Some jars and bottles are designed to be used as something else once they are empty. See how many you can spot in supermarkets and stores.

Chocolate frosting and mustard jars can become drinking glasses.

Vinegar bottles can be used as small jugs for salad dressing.

A coffee jar can become an airtight storage jar.

Ready to refill

Glass jars can be used again and again.

Instead of buying new glass jars of herbs and spices, you could refill empty ones.

Wash small, empty jars and their lids. Use them for storing buttons, paper clips, thumbtacks, or coins.

Try decorating empty jars with painted patterns or glue on paper scraps or old stamps.

Use them as containers for pencils and paintbrushes.

Decorated bottles

In Morocco, some craftsworkers turn all sorts of discarded bottles into something new.

Delightful drizzlers

The craftsmen collect small, empty juice bottles. They cover the base with beaten metal and make a new metal spout and top. The bottles become drizzlers for pouring oil on salads.

juice bottle

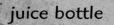

oil drizzler

Silvery sprinklers

Other craftsmen buy old perfume bottles. They decorate them with metal designs and add a new, long, twisted metal spout. These are used as rosewater sprinklers to make rooms smell nice.

perfume bottle ➡ sprinkler

Stunning spice jars

Just by adding a new metal base and lid, medicine jars are changed into spice jars.

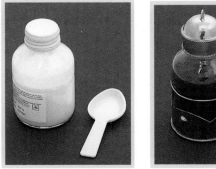

medicine jar ➡ spice jar

Pretty peppershakers

Look how this bottle neck has been turned into a peppershaker. It has a new metal base and lid.

bottle neck ➡ peppershaker

Cut glass

In South Africa, some craftspeople make **tumblers** and vases from empty bottles.

Turning out a tumbler

1. A craftsman scratches a line in a bottle with a sharp cutter, which is set at exactly the right height for a tumbler.

2. He fills the bottle with hot water to the scored line.

3. Then he turns the bottle under cold water, which makes the bottle crack in two.

4. To finish the tumbler, the craftsman smoothes the rough, cut edge.

Two for the price of one

Bottles like those below can be turned into a fine cut glass tumbler and an unusual vase.

The bottom part of the clear bottle becomes the tumbler.

The top part is turned upside down and glued to the upside-down base of the blue bottle.

Look! A new vase.

All change

People have clever ways to reuse things made of glass.

Charming candlesticks

These candlesticks are made from upturned bottles with their bases cut off. The necks stand in a new metal base. The cut rim is trimmed with a ring of metal.

A perfect platter

A whole bottle has been slowly heated and flattened to make this glass plate.

A crazy chandelier

Old drinking glasses and cups are part of this sparkling chandelier. What other pieces of glass can you see? What kitchen utensils can you spot as well?

A green goblet

Can you guess which parts of a bottle were used to make this **goblet**?

Recycling glass

If you do not want to keep old bottles and jars, **recycle** them.

Why bother to recycle?

Recycling glass reduces the amount of waste in landfill. Reusing cullet in the furnace saves taking more raw materials out of the earth to make new glass. Cullet also melts at a lower temperature than raw ingredients, so this saves energy in heating the furnace as well.

Household collection

If your city has a recycling collection program, put out jars and bottles in the box or bag that is provided.

Recycling bins

Otherwise, put glass into recycling bins. Make sure you put each color of glass into the correct recycling bin. Clear glass is recycled into all sorts of containers. Green glass is usually made into wine bottles.

As good as new

More than 30 percent of most bottles and jars are made with recycled glass. There is no difference between a recycled bottle or jar and a new one. Recycled glass is just as clean and pure as new glass.

IT'S A FACT

You cannot recycle every kind of glass. Remember: do NOT put any of these things into recycling bins:

✗ light bulbs
✗ mirrors
✗ glass bowls or cups
✗ heatproof glass dishes

YOU CAN HELP

Before you recycle jars and bottles:

- Empty and rinse them
- Remove any plastic or metal tops and lids
- Sort the bottles by color into clear, brown, and green glass (put blue glass with green glass)
- Put them into strong bags for carrying to the recycling center

Take the bag back home with you and reuse that as well!

New glass from old

Trucks take glass from recycling bins to a **recycling plant**.

Crushed into cullet

Trucks tip their loads onto different colored piles of glass. The glass is put onto a hopper and fed onto a conveyor belt. People then sort the glass by hand, picking out any plastic and cork. Then the glass is crushed into cullet.

Heap of cleaned green cullet

Cullet cleaning

Magnets remove any metal caps or lids from the cullet. Vacuum cleaners suck away paper labels.

Lasers find other waste, such as pottery. Jets of air blow this away. Finally, the cullet is ready for the furnace.

Making bottles

Machines make bottles in two different molds.

1. A **gob** of molten glass drops into the first mold. Air is blown in to create the neck and then the rough shape of a bottle, known as a **parison**.

2. The parison is transferred into the second mold. Air blown into this mold inflates the bottle into its final shape.

parison

bottle

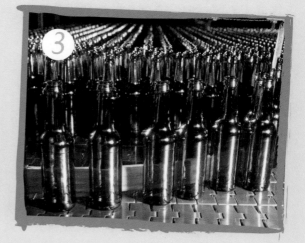

3. If glass cools fast, it becomes **brittle**. To make bottles strong, they are reheated and cooled slowly in a tunnel called a lehr. This process is called annealing.

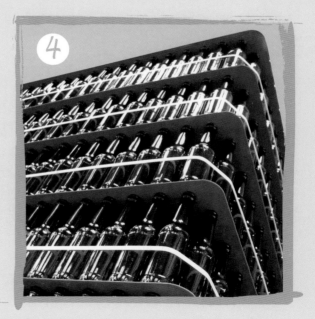

4. The bottles are sent to factories where they are filled, labeled, and capped. Then they are sold to stores.

Glass blowing

In many countries, glassblowers make amazing glass objects.

Making glass by hand

1. The furnace is filled with recycled glass. This is much cheaper than using raw materials.

2. The glassblower picks up a gob of molten glass on the end of an iron tube. He blows down the tube, and the glass forms a bubble.

3. While the glass is still hot, he quickly shapes it with tools. Then he puts it in a cooler part of the furnace to cool slowly.

Really recycled

All of these objects have been hand-blown using 100 percent recycled glass bottles.

This lampshade is made of colored glass balls.

A fruit dish

A vase

A drinking glass

A bowl

Glass galore

People have discovered many ways to recycle glass.

Tumbled glass

Sometimes bottles, TV screen glass, and test tubes are crushed together. The pieces are tumbled to smooth their edges. They are used to make paths, pools, and fountains that glisten and sparkle.

Beautiful beads

Some white glass cosmetic containers are melted and pressed into beads. Tiny amounts of ground metal, called oxides, are added to the molten glass. These color the beads.

cosmetic container

Terrific glass tiles

To make glass tiles, green, brown, blue, and clear bottles are broken into cullet of different sizes—large, medium, or small. The cullet is carefully arranged in square molds. The molds are heated slowly in a kiln. The glass melts just enough for the pieces of cullet to join together into a solid tile block.

Patterned glass tiles like this one have been set at intervals into a pathway to show pedestrians the route to a riverside.

The clear glass tiles shown above were set into the pavement of a town's shopping center. They have lights underneath so they glow at night.

Glossary

brittle easily broken

cullet crushed pieces of waste glass that are recycled

energy the power that drives machines

environment the world around us—the land, sea, and air

factory a building where things are made in large numbers using machines

furnace a large, enclosed oven lined with bricks in which glass or metal is melted at a very high temperature

gob a measured lump of soft, molten glass

goblet a drinking glass with a big cup and a stem

hygienic clean and germ-free

landfill site a huge pit in the ground where crushed garbage is buried

liquid a runny substance, such as water, that has no shape of its own

magnet a piece of iron that has the power to attract steel and other pieces of iron to it

material a substance used to make something else

melt turn from a solid into a liquid

mold a hollowed-out shape; if molten glass is poured into a mold, it takes on the shape of the mold

molten glass hot, melted, liquid glass

natural material a material made by nature, not by people

parison the name given to the first shape of a glass bottle

recycle use an existing object or material to make something new, instead of throwing it away

recycling plant a place where waste glass is delivered and sorted for recycling

reuse use again

rot the natural way a material slowly breaks down into lots of smaller, different substances

sterilize make something completely free of germs

temperature a measure of how hot or cold something is

tumbler a drinking glass with straight sides

Guess what?

- It takes a million years for glass to rot.

- Between 8 and 10 percent of the weight of your household garbage is glass.

- In the United States, about 28 billion glass bottles and jars are thrown away every year.

- A modern glass factory can produce 2,000 bottles a minute.

- The energy saved by recycling one glass bottle will power a computer for 25 minutes.

- Only 32 percent of all glass in the U.S. is currently recycled.

Useful Web sites

http://www.epa.gov/recyclecity/
See how Dumptown became Recycle City with fun games and interesting facts about recycling glass and other materials

http://kid-at-art.com/
Creative art projects to make with recycled materials, and links to other art Web sites

http://www.olliesworld.com/planet/
A fun, interactive site for children, that includes information and tips on recycling plastics and packaging

http://www.planetpals.com/earthday.html
Projects and information about Earth Day, America Recycles Day, and other events that promote recycling

http://www.thomasrecycling.com/kids.html
Tips, facts, and information about recycling

Index